Broken Roses

A poetry book written by:

Oliver Corris

Broken Roses

A collection

Gleaming Dots

by Oliver Corris

Gleaming dots surround the black abyss
above you

Your eyes traveling one by one, in
hopes of seeing only one

Every absent dot you travel, your heart
shatters into a pile of ashes

The ashes covering your once vital soul

Within hours, minutes, seconds, your
heart gives up

The ashes blow away

You can't see him

You never will

For he is one of million gleaming dots

Is it too Late

Is it too late

Is it too late to say I love you

When your heart is miles away from mine

When your eyes are in a separate line

I became numb to the pain, when the rain fell

But now you're gone, and the pain swells

The meaning of love that I now need to redefine

Now is separated and intertwined with the desperation of want

Is it too late to miss your touch

Did I over do it, was I too much

I never meant to ruin what we had

I didn’t mean to become so bad

What we had is ruined now, and my smile is never the same

But my mind is the one to blame

Is it too late

The study of ones hear

Is only the true start

But when one shatters what once was

We go against all the laws

Of what true love may be

Is it too late

Is it too late to say I'm singing alone when the mic is in a different tone

And the batteries are dead

While there’s spinning in my head

Is it too late to hold onto the only thing I know

When my arms can't hold you as I did before

When my hands slip and let go of the love I used
to adore

Is it too late

I Love You

I love you
Why do these words have to be masked?
Why can't I touch my lips to yours without penalty?
Why can't I collide my hands with yours without scowls?
Why can't I love you?

The words expressed giving torment to my spirit
The frowns seen threatening my confidence
The black eyes giving me reminders of my misdeeds
Why do they call love a sin?

I grasp your hand in mine
I kiss your tender lips
I wrap my arms around you
But only in my dreams does it become real

What is Love

Love is a word of lost definition

An unknown language, absent without thought to where it went

No one longer grasps the yearning of warmth within the heart

One of many organs keeping you alive is keeping you from living

Living in a world where love means more

Where when your eyes meet with another's you feel a rhythm in your chest

So why give up now?

Look into someone's eyes and feel their soul meet with yours

Feel someone's hand meet yours in a collision of endearment

Feel what love truly means ve is a word of lost definition

An unknown language, absent without thought to where it went

No one longer grasps the yearning of warmth within the heart

One of many organs keeping you alive is keeping you from living

Living in a world where love means more

Where when your eyes meet with another's you feel a rhythm in your chest

So why give up now?

Look into someone's eyes and feel their soul meet with yours

Feel someone's hand meet yours in a collision of endearment

Feel what love truly means

Time

A dark-shadowed creature suffocates the ill boy
His heart beating like a rapid alarm going off in his chest
The monster covering his spirit with a clawed hand
the boy falling to his brittle knees
His cries for it to stop heard from far
All it takes is time

Radiating torment flowing down his blushed cheeks;
his lungs screaming in pain as his breath refuses to return
his vision fails, his body now a rag doll
his hands dropping to the stained floor;
his body now a vessel for any willing soul,
his heart a destroyed artifact of lost love,
All it takes is time

His lungs a trembling child waiting to be cared for
his tears a symbol of the pain and hurt
The creature, once being a familiar face, now distorted for the worst
All it takes is time

As the weight of the pain grows heavy, the boy stumbles to get up
His previous want for life now growing ill
The creature never leaving as tears escape the boy's eyes like a waterfall of emotions
All it takes is time

Little does the boy know that one day
He will be saved by his own self love
He will be surrounded by his own happiness
He will be worn out by his own playful emotions

Ocean Waves

Waves crash with a collision of intimacy

Loud roars of desire for the warmth of another invade them

Their eyes meet in an instant with a hunger for adoration

Yet they travel apart

Because, after all, who can control love when it is just a crashing wave

True Love

Given the chance I'd kiss your tender lips
I'd hold your soft hands in my own
So why, when given a chance, I don't?
My own heart has proven myself wrong
When all I want is to hold you in my arms
When my heart beats quickly
When my lungs start to forget how to breathe
I fall into an endless hole of utter darkness
Yet there's a bright light shining far below
The light grows as you grow near
Is this love?
As I fall, the light surrounds me
I smile, knowing my time has come
My time to feel love for the first time

Life of a Butterfly

Their wings flap with unforeseen movement
Ignorant to their own potential
They soar through the unaltered sky
As they grow near the luminescent light
Wrinkles arise from their skin
Their eyes begin to sink into an endless void
A void of remembrance
A constant reminder of their past
Their wings start to collapse
Until, at last, they fall.

The Stars

The dullness of the night surrounds my every emotion
Only the light of the moon encompasses the dark
The stars adjacent to the moon, scowling from above
They stare down at me, bitter about my ability of life
I envy them for their lack of it
Every night I am told to give my life to them
Every night I almost do
I take a knotted rope
Yet I untie the noose
I do not cry
Only scream
For the souls of the stars

Blind Eyes

Peer within my eyes
Take a glimpse into insanity
As my eyes no longer see truth
I identify the lies people speak
But integrity makes me blind

Step into my shoes
Glance into the real world
Look at the lies you've told
The lies about your love
The lies about me
Why can't I see your truth?

A Far Away Love

Birds, longing for love, grasping onto any feeling they can get

They are numb, empty

They fly just to feel

The nearly empty sky leaves me unbearably tormented

Tormented by the lack of love I desire

The lack of passion

My fingertips barely able to touch what one would call true love

My heart feels empty without the feeling of adoration

Everyday becomes constant pain

I long for the other half of my heart

My feelings unable to be seen or heard

I long for the feeling of love

But why is it so far?

My Angel

An angel flaps his broken wings
In the hopes that in the end he'll fly
His halo was stolen by the devil
Whom denies him any freedom

People refuse to understand his struggles
He may be an angel but that doesn't mean his life is heaven
He lives with demons in his head
The devil tormenting his heart
The angel tries so hard, yet no one even bats an eye
In the end, he gives in to the voices of the demons
But believe me, my angel,
Life only gets better from here

My Other Half

I stare into the mirror and see myself
But is it me?
I stare into my eyes and see a different soul
Where am I?
The mirror betrays me, showing me an unknown being
Why does it look like me?
My hair, usually curly, is straight
My eyes, showing my own heart, shows another
I look away and realize
It is just my other half, trying to reach privilege
It wants a life it never reached
My other half, who never had a vital
Before passing into another world
Wants to live

The Rhythm of a Broken Heart

A rhythm beats inside my shattered chest

The cracks growing quickly

The rhythm slowing its pace

As a once vivid heart grows still

Until finally it stops

The hurting

The pain

It's gone

The Game of Life
2017

It's all a game

That we all must play.

Our pieces move slowly

On the colorful board.

We earn special achievements as we go

Our pieces move one by one

Depending on the number on the dice

But there is always an end to a board game.

And as we get closer to the end of the board

We remember all the achievements that we earned.

We remember the fun we had while playing

The people who chose to join in the game

As well as remember how long it took to reach the end

And as we take that final step

We smile and take a deep breath

We move our piece one more time

Then rest and put away the game

A burning blush escapes onto my softened cheeks

I hear the echoes of my name ring in your voice

Yet the caves of my heart refuse to let you in

True love, shown to me by one soul
By one thief
Who stole my heart
And I, in disbelief
Wondered, why me?
Your eyes show me creation
While your smile shows me truth
The truth of your elation
The nonexistent happiness residing within you
You, who no longer accepts help, needs honesty
The soul who stole my heart now resides next to me
Displaying what love really is
As I show what happiness can be
The happiness of true love

Broken

Their eyes reflect the memories of a child
Laughing, smiling, but only a mask
Behind it showing their true self
A frown, tears, and shaking hands
Turn into abuse, drugs, and maybe more
When all they know is the world as a hell
Maybe one day they will change
But for now, we hope for the broken

Uncontrollable

He begins to shake furiously

No longer named, he is unknown

He grasps his chest in a swift motion

The doctors seize his arms

He screams, yet nothing comes out

He is empty and numb yet in torment

No one understands his true suffering as they never ask

Are you okay?

He yells for help, yet it never becomes clear

As he shakes, he feels a pinch

Yet nothing happens

He runs, as the doctors never catch up

Because after all, you can't control the uncontrollable

Old Time Love

Thou mustn't live upon the agony of desire

Love and lust, although manifested to be one, must be discrete

The amount of lust one feels mustn't control thy heart

Love is an invisible entry to suffering

And although thou may not place a fingertip on the surface of the torment of love

It will surround thee like a chapped blanket

Only due to what thou call true love

Lust controls most hearts

Cracks only appear on those who let it become one with love.

So, what is love?

Let it Free

Your hand grasps mine in a single move
As you drag me along the gentle sand
The waves of the ocean silent as you speak
The colors of the setting sun illuminating the sharp structure of your face
And reflecting off the tears that drip down your chin
I caress your soft cheek
And the pain you've held so long escapes
The tears rush like a waterfall of torment
Your previously silent screams turn into yells for help
I hold you in my arms
Sheltering you, I whisper in your ear
'Let it out, my love'

Her eyes are like water, pushing me away.
Soft hands grabbing mine in a single wave
I only want what's best, please come this way.
'Cuz all I want is to escape this cave

Don't try to scream or yell, just take my hand
Because all I want to do is try again
So please for my sake, try to take stand
And with your last words, write them with this pen

But don't give up just yet for one day,
You will live in peace up above with him
Just take this gun, but make sure not to say
For one year, it will be completely dim.

Just give me one more chance at this thing love,
So you can fly like a beautiful dove.

One More Drink

Take one drink
It'll be okay
But that's only but a blink
Of what they always say

Take one more hit
You'll feel alright
But just wait till it gets lit
And you won't have much might

They always tell you
To fight what others say
But what if you have no clue
To what you may have to pay

Don't follow the lead
Of those without a life
Even if they plead
Grab out your knife

ISBN 978-1-67800-453-8
90000
9 781678 004538

www.ingramcontent.com/pod-product-compliance
Ingram Content Group UK Ltd.
Pitfield, Milton Keynes, MK11 3LW, UK
UKHW041900190726
13854UKWH00003B/1003

9 781678 004538